Understanding Money

Economies Around the World

Gail Fay

Heinemann Library
Chicago, Illinois

www.heinemannraintree.com
Visit our website to find out more information about Heinemann-Raintree books.

To order:
☎ Phone 888-454-2279
🖥 Visit www.heinemannraintree.com to browse our catalog and order online.

Edited by Megan Cotugno
Designed by Ryan Frieson
Original illustrations © Capstone Global Library, Ltd.
Illustrated by Planman Technologies
Picture research by Mica Brancic
Originated by Capstone Global Library, Ltd.
Printed and bound in the United States of America, North Mankato, MN

15 14 13 12 11
10 9 8 7 6 5 4 3 2

Library of Congress Cataloging-in-Publication Data

Fay, Gail.
  Economies around the world / Gail Fay.
    p. cm.—(Understanding money)
  Includes bibliographical references and index.
  ISBN 978-1-4329-4638-8 (hc)—ISBN 978-1-4329-4645-6 (pb) 1. Money. 2. Economics. 3. Economic policy. I. Title.
  HG220.A2F388 2012
  330.9—dc22   2010038261

112011
006442

Acknowledgments

The author and publishers are grateful to the following for permission to reproduce copyright material:

Alamy pp. 27 (© Kevin Foy), 35 (© Paul Maguire), 37 (© Owe Andersson), 31 (© Megapress); AP/Press Association Images p. 32 (Ariana Cubillos); Corbis pp. 4 (© Jim Richardson), 8 (Hemis/© Rene Mattes, 10 (epa/© Claudio Peri), 25 (© Alain Nogues), 39 (© Yann Arthus-Bertrand); Corbis SABA p. 21 (© Shepard Sherbell); ebay p. 14; Getty Images p. 15 (Washington Post/James A. Parcell); iStockphoto.com pp. 42 top (© Ranplett), 42 middle (© Ufuk Zivana), 43 right (© Joe Gough), 43 left (© Brandon Jennings), 42 bottom (© Joe Gough), 13 top (© Pawel Gaul), 18 (© Andy Dean), 13 bottom (© Andrey Burmakin); Reuters pp. 40 (© Jeff Xu), 29 (© Reinhard Krause); Shutterstock pp. 5 (© Bartlomiej Magierowski), 6 (© Jo Chambers), 16 (© Perfect Illusion), 28, 23 (© Ragne Kabanova)

Cover photograph of Shanghai Skyscraper reproduced with permission of iStockphoto.com (© Nikada).

We would like to thank Michael Miller for his invaluable help in the preparation of this book.

Every effort has been made to contact copyright holders of any material reproduced in this book. Any omissions will be rectified in subsequent printings if notice is given to the publisher.

All the Internet addresses (URLs) given in this book were valid at the time of going to press. However, due to the dynamic nature of the Internet, some addresses may have changed, or sites may have changed or ceased to exist since publication. While the author and Publishers regret any inconvenience this may cause readers, no responsibility for any such changes can be accepted by either the author or the Publishers.

Contents

What Is an Economy?   4

Do All Countries Have the Same Economy?   6

What Is a Free-Market Economy?   10

Which Countries Have a Free-Market Economy?   16

What Is a Command Economy?   20

Which Countries Have a Command Economy?   26

What Is Socialism?   30

Which Countries Have a Socialist Economy?   36

In Focus: What Money Is Used Around the World?   42

Summary   44

Answers to Solve It!   45

Glossary   46

Find Out More   47

Index   48

You can find the answers to the Solve It! questions on page 45.

Some words are shown in bold, **like this**. You can find out what they mean by looking in the glossary on page 46.

What Is an Economy?

The economy is in the news almost every day. It affects you, and you affect it. Every country has an economy. What is this thing called the economy?

An economy is the way a country uses its **resources** to make, sell, and buy goods and services. Goods are things that are made, sold, and purchased. Services are things that one person pays another person to do. There are two parts to the definition of an economy—what a country has and how it uses what it has.

Copper is a natural resource that is taken from the ground, refined, and used to make goods such as electrical wiring and pipes. A copper mine in Utah is shown here.

In factories like this one in China, human resources (workers) use capital resources (tools and machines) to produce electronic goods.

Resources

First, a country's economy is partly based on what resources it has available to use. There are three main types of resources. **Natural resources** include water, oil, soil, wood, precious stones, minerals, and coal. These **raw materials** can be **refined** and processed in order to make things. **Capital resources** include cash or property. Tools, machinery, and computers are examples of property used in manufacturing. **Human resources** are the people who use their skills, intelligence, and ideas in making, selling, and buying. When people are involved in buying things that are made, they are called **consumers**. Consumers are just as important as makers. A country needs to have people who can buy the goods and services it produces.

Goods and services

Second, an economy involves what a country does with its resources. It is how a country uses its resources to produce and distribute goods and services. Goods are items people can buy, such as cars, shoes, or MP3 players. Services are activities that people pay someone else to do for them, such as cutting hair, giving piano lessons, or fixing a leaky faucet.

Do All Countries Have the Same Economy?

Every country's **resource** supply is different. Some countries have many **natural resources** such as oil. Some countries have few high-tech **capital resources** such as computers. Some countries have **human resources** with higher-paying jobs and more money to spend.

Some countries have more capital resources than others. Japan, for example, has a lot of buildings, technology, and machinery to use in its economy.

Each country is also unique in how it uses its resources to make, buy, and sell goods and services. As a result, countries differ in the kinds and amounts of things they produce and sell.

Different economies, same problem

In spite of these differences, all economies face the same basic problem. People have unlimited needs and wants, and there are limited resources available to produce goods and services to satisfy those needs and wants. This problem is called **scarcity**. Because resources are scarce, or limited, each country must decide three things:

1. *What* goods and services should be made and how much?

2. *How* should those goods and services be made (using which resources)?

3. *Who* will consume, or buy, those goods and services?

The answers to these questions are determined by the type of **economic system** a country has.

Solve It!

Goods include items you might buy at the grocery store. If you buy apples at the store, you are buying a good that someone produced. Let's say you buy three pounds of apples for $5, and you give the cashier a $20 bill. How much change would you get? What are different combinations of bills that the cashier might give you?

Needs Versus Wants

Needs are the basics people require for survival, such as food and clothing.

Wants are the extras, such as a skateboard or jewelry.

What is an economic system?

Let's say you are a baker with a limited supply of baking resources. You must decide what to bake, knowing you will have to make a **trade-off**. When you choose to bake one thing, it means you will not have enough supplies, such as flour, to make something else.

Consumers experience opportunity cost, too. When you choose to eat at one restaurant, for example, the cost is missing out on another that you also like.

You think it is important to give people a choice. So you use your resources to make a variety of breads and cookies. Because of **scarcity**, however, you can only make a few of each kind of bread and cookie. This is the **opportunity cost,** or the cost of choosing to make both breads and cookies, instead of making just one item. The cost of making a variety of baked goods is that you can only make a few of each type.

Your friend is also a baker. She thinks it is important to have a lot of her most popular item. She uses her resources to make dozens of cookies. She does not have flour left to make bread, but this opportunity cost is okay because she values amount over variety.

Nations are similar to these bakers. They decide how to use their resources based on what they think is important. The beliefs that guide these decisions make up a country's economic system. A country's economic system determines what products will be produced, how they will be produced, and who will consume them. Today, there are three main types of economic systems: free market, command, and socialist.

Economic Systems

Free-market economies	Command economies	Socialist economies
value more individual freedom and less government interference.	value government-planned use of resources.	value both government planning and individual freedom.

What Is a Free-Market Economy?

A **free-market economy** is a type of **economic system**. It is also called free enterprise or **capitalism**. One central belief of this system is that private citizens may own **capital resources** such as machines and factories, and they may use the **profits** earned from this capital to satisfy their needs and wants. Another value is freedom of choice. Decisions about how **resources** are used are based on these beliefs.

Apple is a business in a free-market economy. The government does not tell Apple what goods to make. When Apple releases a new product, such as the iPhone, consumers are willing to wait in line and pay a lot of money in order to buy it.

Role of the government

In a free market, the government makes few economic decisions. The government does not plan or decide how businesses will use resources to produce goods and services. Instead, these decisions are made by sellers (people making things) and **consumers** (people buying things). Free-market systems are based on the idea that an economy works best if the government does not interfere. This principle is called **laissez-faire**, which is a French word meaning "let do" or "leave alone."

Supply and demand

A free market works by the principle of **supply and demand**. Demand is what the consumers want or need and are willing and able to buy. Supply is the goods and services that sellers are willing and able to make in response to the demand.

In a free market, prices are linked to supply and demand. For example, if many people want the newest video game, demand is strong. Sellers know they can raise prices when demand is high, because people will pay more for that good. However, when the same game is older, demand goes down. When demand goes down, sellers have to lower prices in order to sell the game.

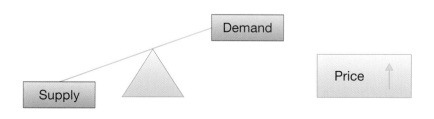

When demand goes up, supply goes down. Seller can raise the price and consumers will pay.

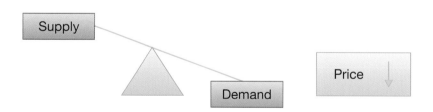

When demand goes down, supply goes up. Seller must lower price in order to sell.

Individual freedom

Freedom of choice is an important part of a free-market system. People can use their own capital resources to start a business to make and sell goods and services. These people are called **entrepreneurs**. Also, consumers can choose where to shop and how much to pay. If consumers do not like the goods or prices in one store, they can shop somewhere else. People are free to own their own property and sell it whenever they want.

Competition

A key feature of a free-market system is competition. For example, Katie can open a fruit smoothie shop down the street from Sam. Katie is free to sell the same kinds of smoothies as Sam. She can set her prices any way she wants. If Katie wants to try to take business from Sam, she can make her prices lower than his. (Competition is strongest when entrepreneurs are free to enter markets when they think they can earn profits and leave markets when they lose money.)

Free-Market Economy

1. *What* should be made?	2. *How* should it be made?	3. *Who* should consume it?
Consumers determine which goods and services will be made. This is demand.	Businesses and entrepreneurs decide how they will meet the demand. This is supply.	People who work to pay for goods and services are the consumers.

Limits

There are limits to freedom in a free market. This is where the government gets involved by creating laws and consequences for illegal economic activity. For example, everyone must pay taxes. Theft is illegal. A person cannot sell alcohol or cigarettes to minors.

If you go to the mall, you will probably find more than one jewelry store. These stores compete with each other to "win" customers. Competition is a key feature of the free-market system.

Advantages of a free-market economy

✓ Individuals are free to own property, start a business, and earn a profit from their hard work.

✓ There are many choices in a free market. Consumers are not limited to one bank or one type of shampoo.

✓ The government stays out of private business. It does not tell people what to make or how to make it.

Disadvantages of a free-market economy

✗ A free market is more risky because businesses are not guaranteed success. For example, entrepreneurs might lose a lot of money if they cannot sell their product or service.

✗ Because there is competition, there might be only one "winner." A big company such as Walmart can offer more choices and lower prices than a small store opened by an entrepreneur. If consumers stop shopping at the small store because they can get better deals at Walmart, the small store will eventually go **bankrupt**.

✗ There is often a big gap between rich and poor. People who work hard or who have more education or ideas earn more money because these abilities are valuable in a free market. People with fewer ideas, less education, or abilities that are not in demand are paid less and thus may end up poor.

Entrepreneurs in a free market can sell goods and services online, too.

Olsson's Books and Records: Competition

Olsson's was a small book and record store in Washington, D.C. The store survived competition from big stores such as Barnes & Noble, but it could not survive competition from iTunes. People started buying music online instead of buying CDs at Olsson's. In September 2008, Olsson's went out of business.

At the same time, however, consumers benefited from this competition. Through iTunes, people had more choices, and they could buy music at a cheaper price from the comfort of their home.

Which Countries Have a Free-Market Economy?

No country today has a completely **free-market economy**. The government often has some influence in economic decisions. There are several countries, however, that mostly run free-market principles such as **supply and demand**. Three examples are Japan, the United Kingdom, and the United States.

Japan

As of 2009, Japan had the fourth-largest economy in the world. This means that Japan is using its **resources** wisely to make and sell goods and services.

Japan does not have many **natural resources**. For example, it has poor soil, so there is not much farming. However, Japan does have a lot of **capital resources**, such as technology and computers, and many **human resources** who can use that technology. As a result, Japan is an industrialized country. This means most of the country's resources are used in making things.

People in Tokyo, Japan, are paid some of the highest **wages** in the world. These **consumers** are able to buy the expensive, high-tech goods that Japanese businesses produce, such as electronics and cars.

Flow of money in the economy

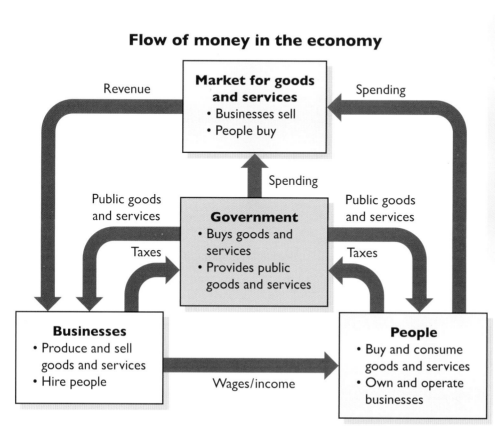

Market for goods and services
- Businesses sell
- People buy

Revenue

Spending

Spending

Public goods and services

Public goods and services

Taxes

Taxes

Government
- Buys goods and services
- Provides public goods and services

Businesses
- Produce and sell goods and services
- Hire people

People
- Buy and consume goods and services
- Own and operate businesses

Wages/income

This flowchart shows how a free-market economy works. **Revenue** refers to income. Public goods and services refer to things the government provides by using money from taxes that people and businesses pay. These include postal service and road repair.

Economy Size

Economy size is measured by **gross domestic product (GDP)**. GDP is the value of all goods and services produced in a country in one year. A higher GDP means a country is using its resources effectively and producing a lot. A lower GDP usually means a country is poor. This could be because the country is not using its resources effectively or it has limited resources to work with.

United Kingdom

As of 2009, the United Kingdom had the seventh-largest economy in the world. About 75 percent, or three-fourths, of the United Kingdom's gross domestic product (GDP) comes from services, not goods. These services include financial (banking), transportation, and hotels. Businesses in the United Kingdom have used available human resources and capital resources to meet this demand for services. **Entrepreneurs**, for example, have opened hotels and sightseeing tours because a lot of people visit the United Kingdom on vacation.

United States

The United States has the largest economy in the world. Its GDP, or total goods and services made in a year, is over $14 trillion. In this free market, business owners and entrepreneurs decide what to produce and how to use available resources. They make some very advanced technology, such as equipment for medical, aerospace, and military uses. Both the national government and individual state governments buy goods and services from these businesses.

Housing Bubble: Supply and Demand

Between 2000 and 2006, banks were charging low fees to borrow money. This made it easy for people to take out a **loan** to buy a house. As a result, the demand for houses went up, and so did the price. Demand and prices kept rising until the bubble "burst." This happened when the low fees suddenly increased, and people could not afford the new loan payment on their home. Many people stopped paying the banks back. The banks took these houses and tried to resell them. Now there was an increased supply of houses. At the same time, it became harder to borrow money. The demand for houses dropped, and so did the prices.

What Is a Command Economy?

Another type of **economic system** is a **command economy**. This system is also known as a planned economy or **communism**. The beliefs that guide a command system are very different from the ones that guide a free market. As a result, the decisions communist countries make about how to use **resources** and how to distribute what is produced are very different from the decisions made in free-market societies.

Role of the government

A command economy is the opposite of a **free-market economy**. The government mostly stays out of the free-market system and lets the laws of **supply and demand** determine products and prices. In a command system, however, the government plans the country's economy. The government decides how to use the country's resources and what to make with those resources. This economic system values equality, so the government takes control to make sure everyone is taken care of and that there is no division between rich and poor.

Lack of freedom

In a true command system, all property and businesses are owned by the government. People cannot become **entrepreneurs**. They are not free to start a business and make a **profit** from it. The government decides which businesses are needed and who will run them, and evenly distributes the profits.

Public Versus Private

Publicly owned businesses belong to the government.	*Privately owned* businesses belong to individuals.

Because the government makes the economic decisions in a command system, people do not have a say in what is produced. **Consumers** generally have fewer options to choose from.

Cooperation, not competition

In a free-market society, people can compete for jobs or open a store just like the one down the street. In a **command economy**, the government emphasizes cooperation, not competition. The government decides what jobs are available and what the **wages** will be. The government also sets prices on things that are made and sold. There is no competition between businesses because all businesses are owned by the government and have the same products and prices.

	Free-Market Economy	Command Economy
What is the government's role?	makes few decisions	makes all decisions
Does the system run by cooperation or competition?	competition	cooperation
Which principle guides the economy: central planning or supply and demand?	supply and demand	central planning
Who owns property and businesses?	individuals	the government
Does the system emphasize individual freedom?	yes	no

Free-market and command economies are based on opposite values and beliefs.

In a communist country such as Cuba, businesses are owned and operated by the government, not entrepreneurs.

Solve It!

Based on what you have read, can you think of one advantage of living in a country with a command economy? Can you think of one disadvantage? Write down your answers before you turn the page.

Advantages of a command economy

✓ Since a command economy is centrally planned by the government, it may be more stable. This means there is less risk of people losing their jobs.

✓ The government uses money from taxes to provide services such as health care and education so that everyone is taken care of, not just people who can afford to buy these things.

✓ There is more equality in incomes and wealth because the government sets wages and evenly distributes its property.

Command Economy

1. *What* should be made?	2. *How* should it be made?	3. *Who* should consume it?
The government decides what will be made and how much. The result is a limited number of choices for the consumer.	The government decides which company will make the goods and services and which resources will be used.	The government decides who needs it and how much consumers will pay.

Disadvantages of a command economy

✗ People have very few choices when they buy goods and services. The government might produce only one type of good, and the consumer has little input into what is produced.

✗ People are not motivated to work hard. If workers know they cannot earn more money by extra effort, what is the point of doing more than they need to?

✗ There is no individual freedom of choice. A person cannot choose to start a new business or buy a home or change jobs.

One value of a command economy is equality. Using tax money, the government provides the same education and health care to everyone.

Which Countries Have a Command Economy?

Before 1991, there were more than 30 countries with a **command economy**. Examples included the Soviet Union, Romania, and Hungary. Over time, most of these countries have decreased the amount of government control and have introduced free-market ideas. Today, there are only two countries in which the government makes most, if not all, economic decisions: Cuba and North Korea.

Cuba

This island country is located south of Florida. Cuba's government is run by General Raul Castro, who took over for his brother, Fidel Castro, in 2008.

Cuba is a **communist** country. The government owns the property and businesses that produce the country's goods and services.

Most Cubans have a poor **standard of living**. This is partly because the government sets their **wages** very low and partly because the government does not use its **resources** to make **luxuries** for people to buy and enjoy, such as air conditioners and DVD players.

In February 2008, Raul Castro started taking steps to improve Cuba's economy. These steps include increasing wages, allowing some Cubans to own their homes, and letting people buy goods such as cell phones, computers, and microwaves, which were previously owned by very few. Also, a small number of people are being allowed to work for a **profit**. For example, hairstylists and people who run small restaurants from their homes are being allowed to set their own prices.

Many Cubans work on **communal** farms, or farms that are owned by groups of people. The government determines how much money people earn at these jobs.

North Korea

The best example of a command economy today can be found in North Korea. This country is located between China and South Korea. Kim Jong-il has ruled North Korea since 1997.

North Korea's government plans every aspect of the country's economy. The government owns all businesses and property, and it makes all decisions regarding production, prices, and wages. Because the government wants the people to be equal in every way, it provides housing, health care, and education to everyone. The government even gives people the same amount of food through food **rations**.

Because of scarcity, all countries must make a **trade-off**. North Korea, for example, spends most of its resources on the military knowing that there will not be money left to produce luxuries that people can buy and enjoy.

Because of its location, North Korea does not have many **natural resources** available to make goods and services. It has a lot of steep mountains, and the soil is not good for farming. The country also has few **capital resources** such as cash and computers. Due to this **scarcity**, the government has to decide what to do with the resources it has. The North Korean government has chosen to spend a lot of money on building up its military. As a result, there is not much left over to improve the standard of living for the people. The government is okay with this **opportunity cost** because it values having a strong military.

Censorship

One result of a controlled economy is **censorship**, or restricting access to information. The North Korean government limits the production and sale of goods and services such as Internet and cell phones. This means most people do not have access to e-mail, websites, or other information from the world outside their country. People do not have the freedom to sell, shop, or look for a job online.

What Is Socialism?

Think about **economic systems** as being dots on a straight line. At one end is the command system, or **communism**, and at the other end is the free market, or **capitalism**. They are opposites. In the middle is a third type of economic system called **socialism**, which has features of the other two systems. In socialist countries, government planning and free-market competition both determine how **resources** are used to make, buy, and sell goods and services.

Command features

As in a **command economy**, the government in socialist countries has a big role in economic decisions. For example, the government controls many important industries such as health care, energy, and public transportation. By owning businesses in these industries, the government can decide what is produced and who should receive the goods and services. The government also determines fair **wages** and sets prices on some products.

In addition, socialism shares the command economy values of equality and cooperation. The government uses tax money to give everyone equal access to health insurance, education, and **welfare** programs.

Vietnam:
A Case Where Socialism Has Succeeded

Vietnam used to be a closed communist country with a command economy. In 1986, the government started introducing free-market ideas such as letting individuals own businesses. Today, Vietnam's economy is more socialist, with both government and individuals making decisions about how to use resources. As a result, Vietnam's **gross domestic product** has grown, people are earning higher wages, and **poverty** has decreased.

Free-market features

Like a **free-market economy**, socialism allows for private ownership of property and business. While the government controls some industries such as transportation, **entrepreneurs** can open restaurants, movie theaters, car dealerships, and many other businesses. The people who own these companies can decide what to make and how much to charge. They can try to make a **profit** and increase personal wealth. This allows for some competition in the economy, and the laws of **supply and demand** have some influence in setting prices.

Even in the government-owned businesses of socialist economies, managers are given more decision-making power than they are in command economies. Managers might be able to hire and fire employees, as well as give a worker an increase in wages if he or she has earned it.

Venezuela: A Case Where Socialism Has Failed

Under the guidance of President Hugo Chavez, Venezuela has become more socialist by increasing government control. Since the mid-2000s, the government has taken over many important industries, including petroleum (oil), tourism, and banking. As a result, the number of privately owned businesses has decreased and so has free-market competition. The **standard of living** for many people has decreased. People have experienced a loss of individual freedoms as well as shortages of food and energy.

Advantages of socialism

✓ The government can provide some regulations and laws to make production and distribution of goods and services effective.

✓ The government can provide programs and services to help the whole population, including the poor, who might not be able to pay for those services in a free-market economy.

✓ Individuals still have the freedom to start their own business and make a profit.

Socialism

1. *What* should be made? Both government and entrepreneurs decide what will be made.	2. *How* should it be made? Both government and entrepreneurs decide what resources will be used.	3. *Who* should consume it? The government decides in some cases, as when it provides college education or health care. In other cases, the **consumer** is the one willing to work for it.

Disadvantages of socialism

✗ In order to pay for public services such as education and pensions, the government takes money out of its citizens' paychecks. These taxes are very high, sometimes 50 to 60 percent of a person's income.

✗ If communism is dominant, people might have fewer freedoms. If capitalism is dominant, there might be more risk of people losing their jobs.

✗ With free-market competition, there is the potential for a big gap between rich and poor. People who work hard or who have more ideas earn higher wages than people who have abilities that are not in demand.

Denmark has a socialist economy. People who live there enjoy a higher standard of living and many government-provided services. However, they also pay the highest taxes in the world.

Which Countries Have a Socialist Economy?

Today, approximately ten countries practice **socialism**. Three examples are included here: Sweden, Norway, and China. Sweden and Norway have based economic decisions on socialism for several decades. China, on the other hand, used to have a strict **command economy** and has recently become more socialist.

Sweden

Scandinavia is a region in northern Europe made up of five countries, the largest of which is Sweden. This country has effectively used socialism to give its citizens one of the highest **standards of living** in the world.

In Sweden's **socialist economy**, the government owns the industries that provide **welfare** benefits such as childcare, old-age **pensions**, and time off when sick. The government spends a large percentage of tax money on health care in particular. As a result, Sweden has one of the highest ranking health care systems in the world, and the benefits are available to everyone. (For advantages and disadvantages of government-provided health care, look at the boxes on pages 37 and 38.)

Sweden also has a strong free market. The country is rich in **human resources** who are skilled workers and use their **capital resources** to start businesses. Privately owned businesses produce approximately 90 percent of Sweden's manufactured goods.

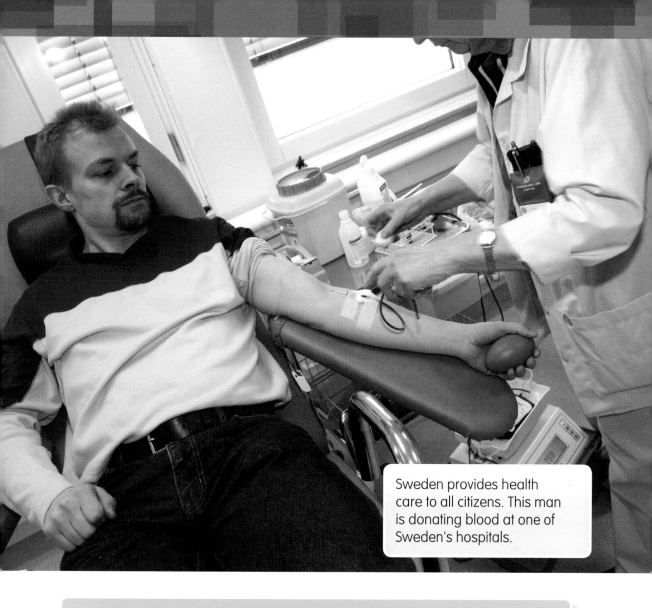

Sweden provides health care to all citizens. This man is donating blood at one of Sweden's hospitals.

Government-Controlled Health Care: Advantages

✓ Everyone has equal access to doctors and medication.

✓ If the government spends a lot of money on health care, people will probably have access to advanced medical technology and well-trained doctors.

Norway

Another country with a successful **socialist economy** is Norway, which is located next to Sweden in Scandinavia. Norway is one of the richest nations in the world in terms of **gross domestic product** divided by the number of citizens. As of 2009, Norway ranked 5th in the world, higher than the United Kingdom (34th) and the United States (11th).

Norway is rich in **natural resources** such as petroleum (oil), fish, and forests. Norway's government has effectively used these resources to make money, or **revenue**, and strengthen the economy. The government controls several key industries, including oil and natural gas. The petroleum industry makes up 30 percent of the state revenue. With this money from oil, Norway has expanded its social welfare programs, which provide hospital care, dental plans, and pensions for use after retirement.

People in Norway have the freedom to become **entrepreneurs** and earn a **profit** from their businesses. As a result, people have a lot of capital resources and enjoy a high standard of living.

Government-Controlled Health Care: Disadvantages

✗ Since everyone has equal access, there are very long waits to see a doctor.

✗ The government decides how much it will pay for medications. If the price is too high, the government may choose a less expensive and possibly less effective medicine. In order to maintain equality, the government may also prevent people from buying the more expensive medicine on their own.

A big part of Norway's economy is based on trade with other countries. They export natural resources such as oil and natural gas.

One out of every five people in the world lives in China!

China

From 1949 to 1978, China was a **communist** country with a **command economy**. Though the communist party is still in power, China's economy has changed a lot. It is now considered socialist, with both government control and private ownership.

In 1979, the government started applying free-market ideas. It broke up the **communal** farms, or farms that were owned by groups of people. The government then gave individual families their own farms, and families were able to keep their profits.

Solve It!

Based on what you have read, which do you think is best: a free-market economy, a command economy, or socialism? List reasons why.

The government also started giving more control to managers of government-owned companies. For the first time, people started receiving pay increases based on how hard they worked. These changes have continued for over 30 years, and many people no longer live in **poverty**. China now has the third-largest economy in the world.

In some economic decisions, China's communist government has more control than the governments of most socialist countries. For example, the Chinese government tells website companies to create jobs for people who will **censor**, or limit, material published online. In this way, the government controls what people can read on the Internet. In addition, each couple is allowed to have only one child. (There is controversy that surrounds this law, though. And, it doesn't apply to all Chinese couples.) China has this limit to control population growth. A bigger population means a bigger problem of **scarcity**, or too many wants and needs to be met by China's limited resources.

What Money Is Used Around the World?

Each country has its own economy and its own money, or **currency**. Many countries use the dollar ($) as their currency. Can you guess which countries use the dollar by looking at the flags below and on the opposite page?

You can find the answers on page 45.

Other countries use different currencies. See if you can match the country to its currency. You can find the answers on page 45.

China	yen
Cuba	pound
Germany	rupee
India	peso
Israel	shilling
Japan	yúan
Kenya	shekel
Saudi Arabia	euro*
United Kingdom	riyal

*As of January 2009, 16 European countries use the euro. They are Austria, Belgium, Cyprus, Finland, France, Greece, Ireland, Italy, Luxembourg, Malta, the Netherlands, Portugal, Slovakia, Slovenia, Spain, and one of the countries in the table above.

Summary

Every country in the world has an economy. **Gross domestic product (GDP)** measures the strength of a country's economy. The dollar amount is the value of all goods and services produced within a nation in one year. A higher GDP means the country is using its **resources** effectively to make a lot of products. It also means the country has **consumers** who have **capital resources** to buy what is produced. A lower GDP means either the country is not using its resources effectively, or the country has very limited **natural**, capital, or **human resources** to work with.

Look at the graph below to compare the 2009 GDP for the countries discussed in this book. Notice that the last two countries, Cuba and North Korea, are quite a bit lower than all the others.

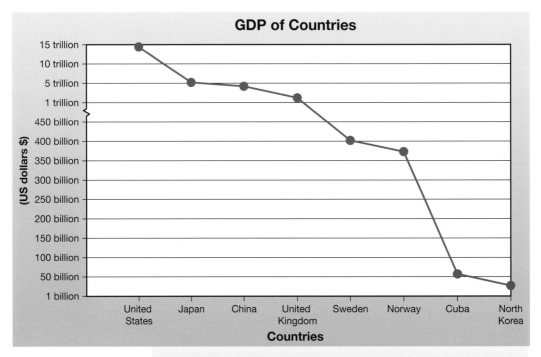

The values in this graph are taken from the CIA World Factbook.

Answers to Solve It! and Currency Quizzes

Page 7:
You will receive $15 in change. Some combinations are: one $10 bill and one $5 bill, *or* one $10 bill and five $1 bills, *or* three $5 bills, *or* two $5 bills and five $1 bills, *or* one $5 and ten $1 bills, *or* fifteen $1 bills

Page 23:
See pages 24–25 for several advantages and disadvantages.

Page 42:
1. Hong Kong, 2. Canada 3. New Zealand 4. United States 5. Australia

Page 43:
China = yúan, Cuba = peso, Germany = euro, India = rupee, Israel = shekel, Japan = yen, Kenya = shilling, Saudi Arabia = riyal, United Kingdom = pound.

Glossary

bankrupt out of money and unable to pay bills

capital resource asset or property that can be used to make and sell goods and services; examples include cash and technology

capitalism type of economic system that values private ownership, competition, and little government involvement; another name for free market

censor limit access to information

command economy type of economic system that values government-planned economic activities; also known as communism

communal shared, owned, or participated in as a group

communism type of political and economic system that values cooperation and communal ownership of property

consumer person who buys and uses goods and services

currency coins and bills used as money in a country

economic system beliefs and values that guide a country's economic decisions

entrepreneur person who starts a business

free-market economy type of economic system that values private ownership, competition, and little government involvement; also called capitalism and free enterprise

gross domestic product (GDP) value of all goods and services made in a country in one year; amount is given in U.S. dollars

human resources supply of human skills, intelligence, and ideas used to make and sell good and services; includes consumers

laissez-faire idea that the government should not interfere with economic activity

loan money lent for a certain amount of time and at a certain fee

luxury an extra; something comforting and enjoyable but not needed for survival

natural resource raw materials that occur in nature and can be used to make and sell goods and services; examples include oil, coal, and natural gas

opportunity cost "cost" of choosing one opportunity over another; cost is based on what is given up when making a decision

pension fixed amount paid to someone, usually after that person retires from a job

poverty not having basic needs met

profit money earned after subtracting expenses; the "extra" someone gets to keep

ration same, limited amount of something, such as food, given to all people

raw material material that can be processed and refined into a different, more usable form

refine to purify and make useable

resource something that can be used to make and sell goods and services

revenue money earned before subtracting expenses

scarcity in economic terms, problem of having limited resources to meet unlimited wants and needs

socialism type of economic system that values both public (government) and private (individual) control of economic decisions

socialist economy *see* socialism

standard of living level of necessities and luxuries enjoyed in everyday life

supply and demand basic principle behind free-market economy; idea that prices are set by the relationship between demand (what consumers want) and supply (the goods and services produced to meet the demand)

trade-off giving up one thing in exchange for something else; results in an opportunity cost

wages money paid to workers; money earned by workers

welfare aid, such as money and necessities, provided by the government

Find Out More

Books

Catel, Patrick. *Graphing Money*. Chicago: Heinemann Library, 2010.

Hall, Alvin. *Show Me the Money: How to Make Cents of Economies*. New York: DK Publishing, 2008.

Orr, Tamra. *A Kid's Guide to the Economy*. Hockessin, DE: Mitchell Lane Publishers, 2010.

Websites

http://www.socialstudiesforkids.com/subjects/economics.htm
This website has information on basic economics, including supply and demand, scarcity, wants versus needs, and more.

https://www.cia.gov/library/publications/the-world-factbook/index.html
The CIA World Factbook has information and statistics about every country in the world.

http://news.bbc.co.uk/2/hi/country_profiles/default.stm
The BBC website has historical, political, and economic information on every country in the world. You can search the profiles by continent, country, and territory.

Index

bankruptcy 14
banks 18

capital resources 5, 6, 10, 12, 16, 18, 29, 36, 38, 44
Castro, Fidel 26
Castro, Raul 26
censorship 29, 41
Chavez, Hugo 33
China 36, 41
choice 9, 10, 12, 14, 15, 24, 25
command economies 9, 20, 22, 24–25, 26, 28–29, 30, 33, 36, 41
communal farms 41
communism. See command economies.
competition 12, 14, 15, 22, 30, 33, 35
consumers 5, 11, 12, 14, 15, 24, 25, 34, 44
cooperation 22, 30
Cuba 26, 44
currencies 43

demand. See supply and demand.

education 14, 24, 28, 30, 34, 35
entrepreneurs 12, 14, 18, 20, 33, 34, 38
equality 20, 24, 28, 30, 38

farming 16, 29, 41
free-market economies 9, 10–14, 15, 16–18, 22, 26, 33, 41

goods 4, 5, 7, 9, 11, 12, 16, 17, 18, 24, 25, 26, 29, 30, 34, 36, 44
government 9, 11, 13, 14, 16, 17, 18, 20, 22, 24, 25, 26, 28, 29, 30, 33, 34, 36, 37, 38, 41
gross domestic product (GDP) 17, 18, 30, 38, 44

health care 24, 28, 30, 34, 36, 37, 38
human resources 5, 6, 14, 16, 18, 36, 44

industrialized countries 16
Internet 29, 41

Japan 16

Kim Jong-il 28

laws 13, 34
loans 18
luxuries 26

military 18, 29

natural resources 5, 6, 16, 29, 38, 44
North Korea 28–29, 44
Norway 36, 38

opportunity cost 9, 29
ownership 10, 12, 14, 20, 22, 26, 28, 30, 33, 34, 36, 41

pensions 35, 36, 38
population control 41
poverty 30, 41
profit 10, 12, 14, 20, 26, 33, 34, 38, 41

risk 14, 24, 35

scarcity 7, 9, 29, 41
services 4, 5, 7, 11, 12, 14, 16, 17, 18, 24, 25, 26, 29, 30, 34, 35, 44
socialist economies 9, 30, 33–35, 36–38, 41
standard of living 26, 29, 33, 36, 38
supply and demand 11, 12, 14, 16, 18, 20, 33
Sweden 36

taxes 13, 17, 24, 30, 35, 36

United Kingdom 18, 38
United States 18, 38

variety 9
Venezuela 33
Vietnam 30

wages 22, 24, 26, 28, 30, 33, 35, 41
welfare programs 30, 36, 38
workers 12, 25, 33, 36